finding Zen, Here and Now

Pause and Reflect

Thejaswini Unni

notionpress.com

INDIA · SINGAPORE · MALAYSIA

Notion Press

Old No. 38, New No. 6
McNichols Road, Chetpet
Chennai - 600 031

First Published by Notion Press 2020
Copyright © Thejaswini Unni 2020
All Rights Reserved.

ISBN 978-1-64783-559-0

Dedication

To all of us who forget
The beauty, grace, and infinite wisdom
In the everydayness of things and your self
This, is a gentle reminder…

Introduction

If you have this book in your hand, it has come to you with hope that you will begin the journey to connect with your self, if not already. In these pages, you will find thirty thoughtful poems that guide you to think more mindfully and appreciate the deliciousness of everyday things, that we are liberally bestowed with.

It is recommended that each poem be read one day at a time, so that your journey to finding zen in the here and now traverses across a whole month (unless it is February of course!).

Each poem is accompanied by a journaling exercise for you to complete. Try to read and journal when relaxed and in a space where you feel at ease. This will help you look within, understand nuances, and thoughts that might not be so explicit in the humdrum of day to day life.

The feather motif that appears across this book represents inner freedom, the boundlessness of the open skies, and graceful guidance.

Be patient with your self, be patient with the universe.
Be inspired by your self, be inspired by the universe.

Finding Zen, Here and Now

1. Familiar Lifelines

Familiarity,
Does not breed contempt.

The chipped, broken mug
From which tea is savoured
Day in and out.

The old man across the street
Who tips his hat when
He sees you,
Perhaps in respect
And you beam out a smile
And love, in return.

The little bird
That dances at your window sill
In hope of nourishment
While nourishing your soul.

The bench you sit on
In the park
Staring at nothing
Yet taking in everything.

The newspaper that you scarcely read
But need to see every day
To know the world has not ended.

Familiarity, on the contrary
For most
Is a lifeline.

Pause and Reflect...

We have some things in our lives that are so closely interwoven with us. A mug, a phone, a bag – they form little extensions of our self.

Write down three things that you think add the warmth of familiarity to your life. What do these mean to you? What are the feelings you associate with these?

2. Explosions All Around

Today,
There could be
An explosion.

A flower may bloom
Defying seasonal odds,
A child may grow up
Neurons firing up to
Understand the world,
Truth may explode
In the face of a thousand lies,
An artist may create
Explosive, intriguing, art.

A million explosions
Surround you every second,
Gifts from life
That have no warning.

Be aware
Embrace them
They are gone too soon.

Pause and Reflect...

Take a few deep breaths and close your eyes. What are the explosions going through you currently?

What thoughts are dominant? What bodily sensations are dominant? Are they trying to tell you something? Have you ignored something for too long?

Write down what are some of the thoughts you discovered? Which ones will you honor today so that you may honor yourself?

3. Studied Silence

Silence watches
As the mango falls
With a thud,

When long-lost friends
Exchange a hug,

As the rain runs
Down the window,

As coffee loses its steam
Waiting,

As the eagle swoops down
on the country mouse,

As ideas turn into
Reality,

When memories
Are discarded without a care,

When the cat stares
In mystery,

When tears fall
And smiles take shape,

Silence rejoices,
As life goes on,
Uninterrupted.

Pause and Reflect...

Sit in silence for some time. In the most crowded place or the most solitary, you have silence within you all the time. How about acknowledging this within you and how it permeates all around you?

Write about your experience with silence. What are some of the thoughts that come up?

4. A Walk

It is necessary
At times
To indulge
In a slow, walking meditation.

Tread softly
With purpose
On the earth below,
As though
Each step
Is part of
A grand, slow dance.

Watch in wonder
Your breath
Slowly moving through you
In no hurry,

Feel with grace
The falling leaf,
The flapping bird,
The blue skies above,

Life tapping its feet
To an unknown rhythm
Playing along
As you walk,
With your self.

Pause and Reflect...

Set aside fifteen minutes today to walk barefoot and mindfully. Notice your deep breath that pulls in energy from the universe. Think about how life goes on around you and follows its own rhythm. Ground and center yourself as you take each step.

Write down how you feel after this walking meditation.

Do you feel more grounded and connected to yourself and the world around you?

5. A Concoction of Choices

As she waits on each table,
At the cafe
Offering a concoction
Of choices
Thoughts swirl up.

Agony from a jilted lover
Crying his heart out,
Hope and fear from
The young man in his first interview
After six months,
Relief and freedom from
The mother of a new-born
meeting an old friend,

Infatuation from the neighbourhood boys chatting
About the neighbourhood girls,
Curiosity from the tourist
Pretending to read a book,
Ambition from the entrepreneur
Delivering his elevator pitch.

They rise up
These thoughts
And dance in wild harmony

As the waitress gracefully swirls
Amidst them
A coffee here,
Some tea there,
A pastry here,
And some cookies there,

A concoction of choices.

Pause and Reflect...

Notice that in any place, everyone has different thoughts, agendas, dreams, and emotions. Each of us are going through our own journeys. Life offers us choices every now and then and it is up to us to choose what really works for us.

What is the choice you are struggling with? How can you accept the struggle and slowly work towards a resolution?

6. The Empty Chair

It was here
A moment ago
The ego
That gave me a form
To preen over,
Clothes to choose,
Shoes to wear,
Manners to adopt,
Cultures to belong,
Company to select,

It sat there
Smug in its construct
Of my self,
Of beliefs and personality,
Of memories to save,
And dreams to conquer,

Just a moment ago
On that now empty chair
Waiting to be dissolved.

Pause and Reflect...

Do you have a place you love to sit at home or in office? A favorite chair, maybe? As you sit there, acknowledge the parts of you which form you. Who are you?

Write down the thoughts that come - what makes you uniquely you. What parts of you are you willing to let go because they no longer serve you positively?

7. Rituals That Make Us

It's age old
This fascination
With rituals

Of days, months
Births and deaths,
Tracking the sun and the stars
Saints and sinners

These natural and man-made
Obsessive, repetitive
Rituals that teach us perhaps
About cycles that can't be changed
And how we attempt to structure
Time's infinite
Lack of structure.

Pause and Reflect...

Ah, Rituals! Take a few minutes to write down the rituals that you identify with in the world – are they family gatherings, meeting with friends, festivals?

What rituals energize and inspire you the most?

8. Faith is Everywhere

To an agnostic,
Faith calls out,

From smiles, from passerbys
A warm meal, in cold times

Coincidences
Crossed paths
Catalysts
The magnificence
Of the night sky
Or mountains or seas,

The outpouring of love
In creating
Art or science,

Faith plays along
At times, a fickle mistress
At times, a life companion.

Pause and Reflect...

At times, we lose faith in ourselves or in the universe. But, there are always little ways the universe signals backs to us not to lose faith completely. That all is well. Life is beautiful.

Think back and write down some moments when this has happened to you and renewed your faith in the universe/ higher power.

9. Light and Life

You will see
That light has all the power
You need to feel alive.

Like the trapped bee in your house
That bangs on the glass window
Driven towards the promise of light.

And in times of rain and thunder
Insects flock to the flickering lamp
At the entrance
Dancing wildly
In warm comfort.

Young saplings will
Lean towards the light
And twist themselves anew
In search for some more sparkle.

And in the morning
As you wake up
Even in the most palatial room
You would want to walk up to the light
Streaming in and radiating on the floor.

It is strange but true
Light gives you all that you need
Even Freedom.

Pause and Reflect...

The power of light is so magical. It illuminates things around us and sometimes illuminates our deepest senses.

What does light mean to you?

10. Days of Poetry

Some days
Are meant to be poetry
Sunlight filtering softly
Through the trees,

Roads that lead nowhere
Leading to a place
Like home,

Love radiating
From every being,

Nourishing tastes
That lighten your step,

The fragrance of trees
Gently wafting by,

And Mother Earth
Reaching out
And holding you in
a soft caress,

Some days
Will stay with you
Forever.

Pause and Reflect...

Poems and poetry are defined as words that stir our imagination and emotions.

Think back to a day or just today – wherever you are. Look at the things around you that nourish you – sunlight, trees, food, the gentle acceptance of mother earth. Bow in gratitude to these that fill your life with poetry.

11. A Mundane Meditation

If the light from the filtered sun,
The hot morning coffee (or tea)
Or the thought of the day ahead
does not awaken you enough,

Let me teach you
A form of silent meditation
My dad taught me
without him ever knowing.

Make your bed...
Like it is your only true possession.

Unfurl the sheet
With all your might
Tuck it in tenderly on all sides
Take your time
Covering corners and sides
Iron out the creases
As though you were relaxing your brow,

Clang the pillows like they were giant cymbals
And then fluff them up softly
Place them side by side,
Or one on top of the other,

Stand back and admire
The inviting form that you just created,
The one that holds your
Dreams and nightmares alike.

Pause and Reflect...

Look at the bed that comforts you and makes way for you every night.

Have you tried making your bed mindfully once you wake up?

Try the bed-making exercise described in the poem and write down how you feel about respecting it and being thankful.

12. Looking for Gentleness

It is rare
Today
This gentleness
The kind that
Reaches another's
Heart.

It does not look
At rich or poor,
Black or white,
Young or old.

There is no respect
For forms or norms,
Structures and definitions.

It comes from
Another place
Deep inside every being,

And it goes back
As the world
Takes over.

Pause and Reflect...

Today, spend some time practising unbiased gentleness. How do you feel about it?

In others, it could often be disguised as kindness or even tentative, timid behavior. How can you help someone gentle who is struggling to express themselves in this world?

13. Before Death

Every day, we die
In a thousand ways
Unannounced, without obituaries.

A thousand cells succumb
To the end, every hour,
Myriad thoughts
As the sun ascends
They dance and die.

There is the death of
Dreams and hopes
And in the outside world
The death of living beings
The last of an endangered species
Must be breathing its last right now.

But, what we are crushed by
Is the death of someone we know
In their physical form
When matter disappears
Our bond with them grows deeper.

A simple "hello" seems in retrospect
to have more meaning
Memories appear from nowhere
Screaming for recognition
We ache to hold on
and play them over and over
In the theatre of the mind.

It is as though death
Gives us the freedom to love,
And be kind,
And pay attention,
And make up for what we
Did not do before.

Pause and Reflect...

Death is a part of everything that is born. It is an eventuality. You would have in your life lost something or someone. Yet, we treat death and its eventuality like it were unknown to us, and when it comes up on us, it leaves us shattered.

Pay respect for a few minutes to those you have lost by writing down your fondest memories of them.

Let us turn our minds to what we can do today to those who are alive around us.

Think of three things you can do to acknowledge the presence of those who are closest to you today.

14. The Goddess of Dawn

Usha
The goddess of dawn
Wakes up early
Spreads her magical
Wings of light
Without fail
Every morning.

Bound by habit,
She gently showers
The earth
With dew
So that grass may
Feel refreshed and
Breathe easy
To welcome the bare feet
That will walk on it.

She then wakes up
Tired mothers
Who have forgotten
That prescribed eight-hour sleep
Who will in turn wake up the
Next generation.

Lovers will slowly
Realize the loved one nearby
And plant a sleepy kiss or two.

From pavement dweller to monarch
Will sit in stunned stupor
Watching her spread this magic.

Fishermen will test their nets,
Entrepreneurs will wish for the next big thing.

As life's expanse comes alive
We slowly
Awaken
From the depths of our dreams,
While the stage for the day
Is carefully arranged
And Usha fades away.

Pause and Reflect...

Have you ever been up at dawn? Is it a task for you to wake up to dawn? For the morning, set an alarm to wake up before daylight just for tomorrow.

Read this poem at dawn and feel the beautiful energy of the morning fill you.

Write down what comes to mind as you take in the promise of a new day or beginning.

15. Every Morning

That first morning cup
Of hot tea or coffee
(A matter of choice)
Is your very own
Oasis for lovemaking.

Stir in sweetness
As much as only you fancy
For the ones who need more warmth
Forget the handle
Hold the cup with both hands
And let gentle heat permeate
Through porcelain
And reach your heart
Caressing it like no other.

Let your soul rise up
And take flight
To wherever
You may wish to go.

Pause and Reflect...

Invariably, we all have a brew we like. For most of us it is that morning cup of coffee or tea. For others, it might just be a glass of water.

What does this morning drink mean to you? Do you drink it in a hurry or are you mindful about it?

As you have your morning cup, think of one dream that you hope will come true soon. Are you working towards it? What can be your next steps to making it come true?

16. Our Life Time

In all this time
Spent living
The clock
ticks second-by-second
a little precision march.

A minute may either
Seem to last an eternity
Or pass away too soon,
Without ceremony.

A day slips away
And begin anew
Rebirthing itself
Out of habit.

Dates, Weeks, and Years
Get marked
On a neatly organized
Calendar.

And you weave together
stich by stich
The charm of daily living,
hopes and dreams,
love and hate
and a million other
threads of human-ness,

Time ticks along
A willing accomplice,
To help you unfurl the
Colourful tapestry
of life.

Pause and Reflect...

Time is our greatest companion in life as it plays along. How tied are you to time?

If you had all the time in the world, what is the one thing you would like to do with your time? Would you like to make a start doing it? It could be learning something new, going for a holiday, or calling an old friend.

Are you ready to make time for time?

17. In Search of Yoga

It is amusing
This yoga
Men and women
With tight sweatpants
Practise in air-conditioned Yogashalas.

Come, take a look at
An ordinary home
Where the mom indulges in
Yoga with focussed devotion
On her children.

Come, see the painter,
Unfurl a million colours
On the canvas, the yoga of his art,

Or watch the pavement dweller share
His only piece of bread with a street dog
The yoga of sacrifice

Do you see the strength in a young athlete
Who is training for a big event he may not win?
His eyes flash the power of yoga.

Yoga might not just be in
physical postures, deep breathing,
or in seeking peace within,

Perhaps it celebrates itself
in devotion,
In form and technique
Of the heart and mind.

Pause and Reflect...

Yoga is everywhere around us. Think of your self. How do
you practice yoga in your daily life – not elaborate asanas or
breathing exercises, but through other simple commitments
to practice and excel.

Is there something you would like to commit to and grow in
your practice? Write down your thoughts as they come up.

18. Free Your Feet

When bare feet
Touch the earth
A connection is made
On the morning dew
That has fallen on grass.

One feels expansive
And stretches the toes
As far as they can possibly go.

When these bare feet
Embrace sand on the beach
They dig deeper
Trying to grow roots
Until gentle water
Comes and washes the sand away.

On hot concrete
They
Get scalded but enjoy
In a masochistic way
To hop or skip
Getting parts of the skin
Warmly toasted.

And then we protect
this natural reaching-out
To earth,
By wrapping them safely
In sock or stocking
And then in shoes
Stilettoes, pumps or wedges
And a thousand other forms.

In which they remain
Suffocated, cramped, frozen
Until later at night
you unwrap them
With an overwhelming
Sense of relief
And let them free.

Pause and Reflect...

Your feet take you everywhere, second only to your mind which has its own travel itinerary. Have you ever acknowledged your feet and the resilience with which they walk this earth?

Write down what you could do for the next few days to show gratitude to your feet. Make time to use them to connect with bare earth.

This exercise in fact lets you deeply think about and honor your entire body.

19. A Key to Desire

When it
Opens your door
You scarcely stop to think
The way this small piece of metal
Controls your entire life.

How it carefully locks away
Parts of you,
Preciously guarding
Your worldly existence.

Those Persian rugs,
The wine glasses
The overflowing bookshelf and
That hammock
And countless other
Reminders of life.

Till you look again
At this magical piece of metal,
Its odd shaped ridges
That has known no beauty
Silently enter the keyhole
And with a dutiful twist
Welcome you home.

Not asking for anything more
Than being a companion
On your journey
Out in the world
Whenever you choose to go.

Pause and Reflect...

Have you ever wondered how something as commonplace as a key can be our greatest possession? It is the same with life. Sometimes, the simplest of things are the most complex. The most deformed, the most beautiful. The more mindful we are of the true nature of things, the more we appreciate the nuances with which life presents itself to us.

Think of a few things that this perspective allows you to identify – what are the things you take for granted that might be very precious to you and in reverse, what are some of the things that are precious to you, which really need not be.

20. Sadness is a Friend

Sadness, my friend
Can be your most precious
Possession
In this world
Where there is really none.

Ask the child
Who lost a toy
The lover who bid goodbye
The athlete
Who lost a race
What does sadness bring?

It brings peaceful quiet
As you withdraw into the
Folds of your own, tender heart
Looking for reserves of strength
Which you are sure to find.

It brings a faint glimmer of hope
That this too shall pass,
A renewed faith in the nature
of time and space
Cyclical versus linear,
It makes you look around
At God's creation and your place in it.

And beyond all,
sadness lets love
Creep into you
When you look at someone else
In this sea of humanity
Experiencing the same.

Hold this sadness therefore
With grace,
Revel in it
When you can,
This precious sadness
For it makes you,
Through a cleansing catharsis,
A better being.

Pause and Reflect...

It is ok to be sad. Too often we are told not to be sad and to put on a happy face instead.

What if instead, we are mindful of our sadness, we acknowledge it within us and let it go?

Write down a few things that make you sad. How can you come to terms when these things happen? How can you overcome sadness and make it a friend? Write your thoughts as they come up.

21. Cold and Warmth

When it is cold
One finds warmth in
Little spots,

The criss-crossing of hands
The inside of elbows
The curve of the waistline
The back of knees,

Treasured amidst cold
Waiting for you to discover them,

Much like how it is
With people or
Places in this expanse,

What a beautiful coincidence.

Pause and Reflect...

Have you ever acknowledged the warmth your own body provides? Irrespective of what is going on outside in the world, there is always a warm place to be in – your own self.

Take a few minutes to touch parts of yourself that are the warmest.

Write down areas where you feel this warmth is running freely and nourishing you.

22. The Depth of Life

Did anyone tell you
Life is short?
I hope you did
Not pay no attention.

Because life is neither
Short nor long,
It only expands deeply,
The depth of
What you Experience,
In the deep, vastness
Of your conscious self.

The depth of love
That rattles your heart,
The depth of dreams
That propel you forward,
The deep, murky waters of
Hate, pride, jealousy,
The depth with which you
Breathe, laugh, dance,
The depth of light
From the sun, the moon, the stars.

It's really always
About the depth,
Which is
Immeasurable in time.

Pause and Reflect...

Life is deep in so many ways only if we mindfully turn our attention to it.

Think of two or three instances where it you experienced the depth of life in a person, place, or thing. What are your thoughts around that experience?

23. When Night Falls

Let's for once
Talk about the night,
Ignored for too long
While we fall for the glory
Of each morning.

The night gathers
Weary souls
To rest and retreat
Into the world of dreams.

In the pure sanctity of night,
the midnight oil burns
Casting a faint glow
And bringing warmth
Of an unknown kind.

Those who roam at night
Walk with the moon and stars
As willing companions
Their obscurity protected
Amongst shadows.

Lovers exchange passion
Like a token before
the morning haste.

Crickets chirp to
A strange song
Fireflies go on with
Their dancing.

As you use the night to
Cleanse with tears
Or revel in celebration
Unassuming,
With no claim to fame,
It lets you wait
In relaxed anticipation
For the morning.

Pause and Reflect...

As you sleep today and leave the weariness of the day that has gone by, think about the beauty of the night that comes at the end of every day and allows you to rest.

Write down your thoughts as they come to you, about the relaxing care of the night.

24. What Flowers Tell Us

Today,
Bring home some flowers.

If you are lucky
Those that have freshly fallen,
As they lie after death
Kissing the earth,
Or from a florist
Who will create his own art
In minutes.

Give them a new home
A vase of glass
Or porcelain,
Maybe, even a small tray.

Slowly,
Add life-giving water
As though you want to wake them up
From their deep slumber.

For days from now,
Watch their glory
Rise up
And fall again.

A beautiful reminder
Of life and
Its fragility.

Pause and Reflect...

Like flowers, life blooms and then fades away. Every moment is brought to us with a potential to be made the best of.

Write down three things you would do to be mindful and help fully bloom in your life. It could be working on aspects of yourself, friends and family, or something to sharpen at work.

25. Remembering the Womb

I have a fleeting
memory
Of being within
A warm space
Enveloped by a gentle
Rocking ocean.

I slept without haste
Through days and nights
Feeling a heartbeat
Not very far from my own
Like a clock ticking to remind me
Where I was.

I dreamt of lives past and,
Lives to come
From one realm to the other,
A blinding trail of colors.

And from this deep, beautiful
Space of rest,
I was soon born
As a gift of creation,
Into arms that held me
As though they had waited
Too long.

My eyes opened and
The journey began.

Pause and Reflect...

We forget the womb as soon as we are born and start our life journey. However, we somehow ache for the comfort of a closed, protected, safe space throughout our life. Let us for a moment be mindful of our mother's womb and the warmth and safety it provided us, for nourishing us and for allowing the universal life force to light its spark in us.

Write down thoughts that come up and whether we are truly thankful to our mother. Are there any closures required that prevent you from doing so? What is the inner clearing work that is required to be done?

26. Roads Ahead

A road
Is always
Part promise, part hope
Leading you somewhere
And then everywhere.

It has
Endless stories to tell
Witness to lives and deaths,
To eloping lovers,
And sons and daughters
Returning home,
To the high-speed chase
And the odd breakdown,
To merchants
And musicians.

You take the road ahead
Not by choice
But as the only option
To discover what lies beyond.

That sharp curve
The steep incline
Or beyond the seemingly
Endless straight line.

The road is where
Some of us truly belong.

Pause and Reflect...

Roads always represent promise. We always refer to the path ahead and the journey of life.

Using this metaphor, what are some of the roads you want to traverse? Are you comfortable in the one you are in now? What will enable you to fully enjoy this journey? Mindfully, put down your thoughts and goals.

27. Smiling at Strangers

It has come to me
After years of a
Serious visage
This carefree
Smiling at strangers.

As I see you
Walk up
And know you will
Look at me,
Much to my surprise
My lips begin to
Dance, curl, and spread
Themselves into
A smile.

A little shy,
a little unsure
And I see you,
the God in you
Go through the same
Involuntary action.

Our shy, unsure smiles
(For those few seconds
And in a way
That cannot be explained)
Make a connection
That is beyond us
And our ordinary lives.

This makes my day
And I hope it will make, yours.

Pause and Reflect...

Have you smiled at strangers and initiated a conversation?
Why don't you do one today?

What were your feelings as you did this? How did it make
you feel? How do you think the other person felt?

28. The Story of Bread

When bread rises
Its aroma
Tells you your own story
Of what it means to you.

It reminds you
Of the warmth
Only a meal with bread
Can provide.

It hints at equality,
Be it bread rising
On a small girdle (The roti)
In a small hut
Far away from
Modern comforts
Watched over with loving eyes
And deft hands
Creating the only meal
they will have,

Or bread rising
In the most state-of-art
Michelin-star restaurant
Served as free carbs
To break bread.

It overwhelms you
With patience
Where you can't hurry
Some things
Even as simple as bread.

And it assures you
As you pass by and
It wafts down from
Somewhere,
That all is well with the world.

For bread is being made
And it is rising.

Pause and Reflect...

Bread is so fundamental in most cultures. Rice holds the same stature in rice-eating cultures across the world. Irrespective of where you are from, think about what food means to you.

What does your comfort food bring up in you – what feelings or emotions are associated with it? What memories get stirred?

29. Creating Connections

From the time, it
Starts Its journey
Up or down
Punctuated by stops
To collect more souls,

It holds inside
Like a heart about to burst
Expressions and thoughts
No two ever alike
(Really no way to know),

Creating
Relationships that last only for
A stolen glance
Or a warm Good Morning.

It's a wonder
How the small space
Inside elevators
And the smaller journey
Sometimes can create
A warm
Connection.

Pause and Reflect...

Have you ever been up and down an elevator, especially on your way to work? How does the momentary connection in the elevator feel? This can be applied to all public places – parks, movie halls, fitness centres, or bazaars.

What does it mean for you to be part of a community of human beings? What do you think is your role in it? When you are connected to a larger group of people, what are some of the things you discover about yourself?

30. Miracles Around

Today,
If you have been
Waiting for a miracle
To lift you up
From the quagmire
Of daily living,

Caress the soft
Deep colours of a petal
And how they come together
To form a perfect flower,

Gaze at the clouds
Of cotton dotting the sky
Changing shape
As they drift by,

Watch water run along
Gurgling, cleansing,
Not wary of what it flows through,

Listen to the soundless
Flow of air
Around you
Stoking trees, rustling leaves
And in you, as
Life-giving breath.

Today,
Just pay attention
To the miracles
Around you
And you will need no more.

Pause and Reflect...

There are so many miracles unfolding around us that we scarcely notice. Slow down and acknowledge some of them.

Identify your private go-to miracles so that you can use them as an anchor to come back to, when things go wrong or something is just not right.

Congratulations!

Hope you had an interesting journey appreciating how zen is interwoven into our everyday life and how a little reflection can help you connect with your deepest self.

At times, you might not have experienced any shift and that is completely ok. This is just the beginning. As long as in days to come, you experience life a little more deeply and are able to appreciate your place in this world, the inner journey has begun.

At any time, when you feel stuck, disappointed, or are struggling for answers, go back to the book or any of the poems and exercises to help you move ahead.

Be patient with your self, be patient with the universe.
Be inspired by your self, be inspired by the universe.

CPSIA information can be obtained
at www.ICGtesting.com
Printed in the USA
BVHW070832110920
588365BV00004B/247